D1629858

HOCUS POCUS

TITANIA'S BOOK OF SPELLS

HOCUS POCUS

TITANIA'S BOOK OF SPELLS

TITANIA HARDIE

PHOTOGRAPHS BY SARA MORRIS

QUADRILLE PUBLISHING

This is dedicated to Samantha 'Pook', and Oberon;
and especially to my aunt, Zena Sambrook, 1907-1995:

'Love seeketh not itself to please,
Nor for itself hath any care,
But for another gives its ease,
And builds a Heaven in Hell's despair'

William Blake

Publishing Director Anne Furniss

Design Johnson Banks

Production Vincent Smith

First published in 1996 by Quadrille Publishing Ltd,
9 Irving Street, London WC2H 7AT

© Text Titania Hardie 1996

© Photographs Sara Morris 1996

© Layout and design Quadrille Publishing Ltd 1996

All rights reserved. No part of this book may be reproduced
in any manner whatsoever without permission in
writing from the publisher.

British Library Cataloguing in Publication Data
A catalogue record for this book is available from the British Library

ISBN 1 899988 01 7

Printed and bound by Arnoldo Mondadori Editore spa, Verona, Italy

An Introduction to Magic

To admit the possibility of magic in these cynical days requires almost a child-like faith. To accept that potions, brews or chanted rhymes can positively alter our circumstances must necessarily suggest a return to the days when we listened to fairy tales and expected that everything would turn out well in the end if you really believed it would. As adults we dismiss this belief as foolish and irrational. We have learnt that money doesn't grow on trees, that it is impossible to find the end of a rainbow, never mind the pot of gold, and that kissing any number of frogs is unlikely to yield anything more than a wart on the lip. None of this, however, appears to diminish our curiosity and insatiable interest in life's mysteries. Even though we live in a rational world where science attempts to provide an answer to every question, we continue to be fascinated by subjects which seem to elude a straightforward scientific explanation, such as the existence of ghosts, UFO sightings, the miraculous recovery of supposedly terminally ill patients, or the accuracy of clairvoyance. This must be because we want to inhabit a world where there are still some unknowns, where there remains a place for faith itself. To believe in magic as a viable way of enhancing our quality of life does require a leap of faith. We must see life in slightly romantic terms: recognise falling in love or growing a flower or even cooking a perfect pie as a demonstration of the magic of balance, of everything coming together in just the right way. For, however scientifically our chemical responses can be analysed, no one has ever successfully explained the phenomenon of love to me. If magic can be defined as it is in the dictionary simply as '...the use of ceremonies, charms and spells ... to produce or prevent a particular result', there is nothing so very extraordinary about it. It works on the simple premise that by harnessing the power of concentration (the force of the 'wish-power') and combining it with the clever use of herbs (which are known to have complex chemical properties) and other ingredients, we can change the way we are perceived by others, improve our health or boost our confidence, all with beneficial and lasting effects. This marriage of the spirit and the psyche to physical ritual and treatment has a long history. Until the seventeenth century, all doctors were aware that the physical healing of the body with herbs or any other treatment would not be successful unless the spirit was also healed, as the physical and spiritual self were known to be closely connected. Elaborate instructions were given in herbals for gathering herbs at a particular time of day or cycle of the moon (factors which again are now being 'scientifically proved' to change their properties) and always the promise of cure came carefully annotated with words such as 'and with God's will...', to remind us that faith was a prerequisite in healing. It is only now, three centuries later, (apparently thanks to the results of 'scientific experiment') that we are beginning to return to the belief that mind, body and spirit are indivisibly interlinked, that all three must work together to effect a change.

With this in mind, the reader should set out to test the efficacy of magic with the help of the spells that follow. There is no need to become an apprentice witch or espouse the pagan philosophy, but there are rules for working magic that should be adhered to. Always remember that you must exercise caution with magic: the ingredients you use may come from the garden or the kitchen, but it is nevertheless a powerful tool. You have a moral obligation never to use it to hurt or gain control over someone else. Use it instead as your own secret weapon – like wearing a wonderbra or a fabulous designer fragrance. His expertise in magic endowed Merlin with a charisma as tangible as that of the king he served. If as a result of performing your spell you feel that you've taken more control of your life, and therefore feel better about yourself, you've won half the battle.

Tools of the trade

If the thought of working magic spells has given you half a mind to scan mail order catalogues in pursuit of a cauldron, don't be hasty: it is by no means essential that you have one. The stuff of making spells is perfectly accessible to anyone. It might seem disappointing to discover that most of the ingredients you will need for your magic can be purchased at a good supermarket, but there is really no need to make difficulties where there are none. It is true that many people feel their magic is imbued with greater strength and mystery if certain ingredients are 'gathered by moonlight', or require long journeys to a supplier of herbs or oils. If this works for you then you should be encouraged to continue, instigating a treasure hunt for the items needed for a spell. Certainly, it helps to create a good atmosphere and level of concentration for performing magic if there has been a sense of ceremony in the collection of the items. Most of the objects used in spells are rather ordinary – it is what you do with them, and how you 'charm' them, that will turn an ordinary dinner candle into a magic wand, or a casserole dish into a cauldron. If your mind is strong and your heart pure your magic-making will have an excellent chance of success without much preliminary ritual; but if you want to give your spells their best chance of working, take time to get the right tools together and to understand the psychological concepts of working magic. Any effort you spend in creating the right mood, preparing the area you'll work in and learning how to work with the tides of the moon is effort well spent. It is also wise to stock the larder with a few useful items that you will need on a regular basis.

🐱 A CLEVER WITCH'S SUPERMARKET TROLLEY WILL MAKE STRAIGHT FOR THE SUPPLIES OF FRESH HERBS IN STOCK, TAKING ADVANTAGE OF WHAT IS IN SEASON BEFORE DECIDING ON WHICH SPELL TO PERFORM TO ACHIEVE HER GOAL. If basil is abundant and you want to do a love spell, the ingredient might be said to make the choice of spell for you. Garlic and, indeed, basil are used over and over in magic (and have the added advantage that they can be whisked up into a pesto sauce if you're caught on the hop with unexpected dinner guests). Mint, marjoram and verbena now also belong in your pantry. If your windowsill permits and you can grow them fresh, all to the good. Always buy fresh herbs if they're available and dry them yourself if need be. The use of herbs in magic is, as with cooking, all the more powerful if the ingredients are fresh; but sometimes this will not be possible, and dried herbs can then be used with complete confidence. 🐱 CANDLES OF ANY COLOUR WILL NEVER GO TO WASTE IN A WITCH'S HOUSE. Used repeatedly in spells for love, health, luck and money, you will also never fear power failures again if you keep a good supply. Choose white and red to keep in a cupboard for emergencies and buy pink, green, and lavender for more specialised needs. Whenever possible buy scented candles, which set the atmosphere for magic as well as having many uses in healing. 🐱 IN THE BEVERAGES AISLE, STOP AND SEE WHAT HERBAL TEAS ARE ON OFFER. Camomile, vervain, elderflower and peppermint make excellent bases for love and healing potions to which other ingredients can be added. Pop into the next aisle to find the honey, an absolute must for spells. In the wine section, choose whatever your budget will allow; bubbles have the most value to a witch, but any strong wine can form the basis of your brew. Wines are also used in ceremonial toasts, demonstrating that witchcraft has much in common with other spiritual ideologies. 🐱 ONE OF THE MOST IMPORTANT ITEMS YOU WILL NEED IS A RED CORD OR RIBBON – more helpful than a crystal ball for putting you in touch with the spirits. You will use it again and again for thought transference and contacting people, but it is important to use good-quality ribbon – gift wrap ribbons have entirely the wrong feel, so a visit to the haberdasher's is recommended here. Buy several metres, but cut a special length of one metre which will become your personal message line. 🐱 CERTAIN OILS ARE UTTERLY ESSENTIAL TO THE WORKINGS OF SPELLS, SO BUILD UP A LITTLE CACHE OF THEM. Lavender is matchless in magic, exciting the passions, calming the senses, useful in first aid as well as enchanting everyone's olfactory senses. Thyme oil is time-honoured, lemon and lime oils will be needed and rose and geranium can be used in a multitude of ways. The best oil for getting your brain into gear is rosemary, which again has a dozen applications. These, then, should be the core of your collection.

🐱 Two items are absolutely essential. Buy a small knife of good quality, tie its handle with a white or red ribbon and hold it up to the moon on the first night you bring it home to charge it with gentle lunar energy. Use it to cut flowers and herbs for spells, but use it only for magic. The other vital component is a candle holder which you will reserve for the burning of magic candles. Make it a special, noble object – something which satisfies you aesthetically but is also strong, solid and won't tip over. Glass is beautiful, but metal would be both representative of the elements and more durable as well. Silver is an excellent choice, as it is the precious metal of the moon. 🐱 Traditionally, witches have used their emblematic 'besom', or broom, as part of the working of their spells. The role of this household item is to sweep away and cleanse the environment for performing a spell, as well as to rid the house of negative thoughts from other people. Brooms not being as common as they once were, the contemporary magic-maker might prefer to use a vacuum cleaner – the same results can be achieved. 🐱 The other quintessential witch's companion, or 'familiar', the black cat, is very much a matter of personal choice. I keep a white rabbit as a pet and though he deports himself like a cat and naps in front of the fire, I don't think of him as my familiar and in truth pets have no particular role in magic spells. 🐱 A magic mirror will be useful for putting your own 'stamp' on a spell, and to reflect the moon's light, thus invoking her grace and blessing on your work. Choose a hand mirror about 15-20 cm in diameter and charge it with the rays of the first full moon after you've bought it. Keep it in a dark-coloured bag when you're not using it. 🐱 Lastly, you will need a heatproof container for mixing your brews and potions. A saucepan is fine, a kettle would do, but for sheer theatricality you can't beat a cauldron! If such a thing could be fitted into your life without causing alarm to your friends and neighbours, then make your purchase. Otherwise, opt for a cast iron pan or casserole dish. You will not need it for anything sinister, but there will be the odd spell where nothing else will have quite the same effect.

Harnessing the elements 🐱 So much for your equipment list. There now

follow one or two tips for good spell-making. Whenever possible, think about the phase of the moon at the time. There is a full list of the witch's moons in the appendix, which will give the more historically minded a background for performing magic by the moon. But even if you're not concerned about which of the famous thirteen moons is currently in the sky, try to be aware of whether the moon is waxing (growing towards full) or waning. The full moon is the most powerful, but a waxing moon is desirable to work by if you want to attract something to you, whereas the waning moon is the best choice for ridding yourself of anything negative (be it a callous lover or a bad head cold).

For working up a truly powerful spell, consider the weather. If it is foggy, your spell will be unable to travel far or fast through the ether; if it is rainy, you may feel a bit down (although water is an excellent medium for carrying magical thought); but best of all, a far cry from a sunny day, you can't improve on stormy weather for making magic. When all the electricity is flashing about in lightning storms and when thunder reminds us how sound carries across the earth, capitalise on the moment and get out your spell book. Borrow from the energy of the storm to charge your own battery, and you'll be amazed at the strength of your incantations.

Learning the art of magic

For all your magic-working it is essential that your mind be focused, by a self-induced meditative state, or even a touch of self-hypnosis. Everyone can do this but, like swimming or playing the violin, it takes practice. Some people take to it very easily, and they will find it easier to make their magic work quickly and well than those who have to struggle a bit. The best way to learn to focus is to try the following exercises, which will train your mind to hold one thought for a long time. Try making a candle flame burn higher and lower with the energy of your mind. Stare at the flame and tell it to burn higher, higher, until you see some movement. It may take a few goes, but eventually the candle flame seems to obey your every command. Another excellent exercise is to try sending a friend a message at a particular time every day. Choose someone you're very close to, and don't tell them what you're doing, but see if after a few days he or she tells you you've been on her mind. Remember, these exercises require practice, so don't give in if nothing seems to happen for a few weeks. You are training your mind to a particular task it is unfamiliar with, and like any other lazy muscle in your body it takes a great deal of flexing to make it work at peak performance. But keep trying; you can do it if you persevere. Many of the spells in the book ask you to send a 'beam of white light' either around the room you're working in, or perhaps to another person. This is a simple procedure but again takes some practice. You must imagine as vividly as possible that a tornado of white light is stirring from within the room, and imagine it spiralling around and around, in a clockwise direction, so that it reaches into every corner of the room and cleanses and energises the area. This may make you feel quite weary the first few times you attempt it, but after a while you will find you are recharged and vibrant yourself from the activity. Sustain the circling motion of the light in your mind for a good five minutes, and use this routinely to protect your home and your family, rid yourself of doubts and negativity, and to contact friends or send help to someone in distress.

A FRIEND WHO HAD TO DELIVER THE EULOGY AT THE FUNERAL OF A SISTER WHO HAD DIED UNEXPECTEDLY TOLD ME OF THE OVERWHELMING FEELING OF 'RESCUE' HE HAD RECEIVED WHEN MANY OF US IN THE CONGREGATION HAD ENCIRCLED HIM WITH LIGHT TO HELP HIM THROUGH HIS EMOTIONAL ORDEAL. He described it as feeling flooded with white light, almost as though angels were lifting him high. Certainly, it can be a very powerful energy source. THIS BRINGS US TO THE LAST POINT: A PLACE TO PERFORM YOUR MAGIC. It is not necessary to have one spot in particular, but choose a time and location where you will not be disturbed. If the wrong person walks in on you, you'll either have a lot of explaining to do or possibly even find yourself tied to each other in a new (and not perhaps desirable) way! For the most part magic should be private, so perform your spells as you would say a prayer, somewhere quiet where you can concentrate your thoughts without distraction. IF CALLED UPON TO CREATE AN 'ALTAR' FOR A SPECIFIC SPELL (WHICH YOU MAY IN FACT DO AS A MATTER OF COURSE IN ALL YOUR SPELLS) DO THIS AS YOU WOULD LAY ANY SPECIAL TABLE. Place a cloth upon the surface, deck it with flowers appropriate to the subject (most spells will specify) and light a candle: usually white, but sometimes another colour, including pink for love, red or lavender for passion, green for healing and so on. The appendix contains a list of gods and goddesses whom you may choose to dedicate your altar to: this is a matter of personal choice. NOW YOU ARE READY TO START YOUR SPELL-MAKING; BUT FIRST, REMEMBER TO EXAMINE YOUR MOTIVES AND MAKE SURE YOU ARE PERFORMING YOUR SPELL WITHOUT TRYING TO FORCE ANYONE INTO SOMETHING WITH WHICH THEY WOULD NOT BE COMFORTABLE. Don't violate your good strength or their free will. Magic is like an irresistible invitation, but it should be used to draw, not force, others into a happy contributory role in your life.

FIRST
FIND YOUR
PRINCE

1

A SELECTION OF SPELLS FOR ATTRACTING LOVE.
With the first flush of a new love you truly seem to
walk a few inches off the ground. There is nothing
quite like it ~ no more wonderful time to be alive.
If you are still waiting for someone special, or if
you've finished with someone else and are ready to
paint the town red again with a new partner, try any,
or all, of the next few spells.

Sowing the seed of love

❧ To attract a special lover. No-one could teach the world more about love than the Italians. To follow a custom my Italian grandmother taught my mother (and in the same tradition as Isabella's pot of basil in Keats' poem) this spell demonstrates how pouring your love into a little basil plant will ensure a strong love with someone.

You will need

A small pot; some earth; some basil seeds

❧ On a waxing moon in late spring or summer, take a few basil seeds and sow them carefully in one or two small pots or containers; as you sow them, sing a sweet song or think loving thoughts, and feel love entering your life. Water the seeds lovingly each day until they germinate, saying as you do: *'Sono innamorata. Grazie'*. When the seedlings appear, take great care of them, especially if the weather is cold (in which case you will need a very sunny draught-free window). You mustn't let them die and never use these special plants for cooking, for they are sacred to love. ❧ You will meet a special love within a few months – perhaps the love of your life.

My good friend and former neighbour, Zoe, did this spell to excellent effect many years ago, just before she met her present husband. She chose a Greek yoghurt pot for the container; rather amazingly, when she met him she discovered he had lived for many years in Greece. We did our magic together and she nursed the seedlings on her sunny windowsill. The power must have been strong, for I, too, met my future husband a few months later.

Crowning glory ♥

A SEDUCTIVE HAIR RINSE TO ATTRACT ATTENTION. The Irish, too, have some wise words on the subject of love. This hair tonic, conceived in the days before designer shampoos, makes your hair gleam and bewitches everyone with the intoxicating smell of your tresses.

YOU WILL NEED

1 tablespoon orris root; 1/2 cup finely chopped parsley; 1/2 cup macerated lavender flowers

♥ AFTER SHAMPOOING YOUR HAIR BEFORE A PARTY OR A DATE, STIR THE INGREDIENTS INTO A CUP OF WARM SPRING WATER TO MAKE A RINSE. Let it steep for half an hour and use after or in place of conditioner. You will be delighted with the effects as you attract attention like bees to nectar!

Wreathed in smiles ♥

To BRING SUNSHINE INTO YOUR LIFE. Another beautiful spell for the hair can be worked at the height of summer, when glorious sunflowers are in full bloom. If you can put aside an hour on a sunny Sunday, this spell is ideal for a daytime date.

YOU WILL NEED

A few drops of sunflower oil; 7 sunflowers; 1 metre of yellow ribbon

♥ BEFORE GOING OUT TO A DAYTIME OCCASION, SUCH AS SUNDAY LUNCH, MASSAGE A FEW DROPS OF SUNFLOWER OIL INTO YOUR SCALP AND THE ENDS OF YOUR HAIR. Make a circle on the ground with the sunflowers and lie with your hair inside the circle in the full sunshine. Chant to the Archangel Michael, or Helios, to send down a love for you during the sunlight hours which come under his dominion, then close your eyes and try to see the face of the one who will be yours through the light of your lashes. Sit up, wind the yellow ribbon around your right forefinger, place it to your 'third eye' (between your brows) and ask again for a new love to bring sunshine into your life. Concentrate for a few minutes, then unwind the ribbon. ♥ WASH THE OIL OUT OF YOUR HAIR, TIE THE YELLOW RIBBON AROUND YOUR HEAD AND SECURE THE FLOWERS BENEATH THE BAND TO MAKE A FLOWERY HEAD-DRESS. Say out loud the names of the seven days of the week, and wear the wreath on your date. ♥ WITHIN THE WEEK, YOU SHOULD HAVE MET SOMEONE WITH A SUNNY PERSONALITY.

A seashore spell ❧ To attract a foreign lover. There has always been something glamorous and superior about a love affair with a foreigner. If you have drunk from the cup of holiday romance but prefer that, this time, he should come to you, plan a trip to the seaside, and see what you can do to influence the fates.

You will need

A sea shell; a lock of hair; a small silver charm; a sprig of rosemary; a small piece of paper; a red ribbon or cord;
sealing wax; a flask of wine; your magic mirror; matches

❧ When the moon is newest and the evening long, journey to a quiet seashore. In a pouch carry the above, tokens of your love, and at day's end sit by the water's edge facing the rising moon. Breathe in the salty fragrance and imagine your life filled with love, with the partner you hope might be your companion. Hold the talismans in your outstretched hands: the shell, symbol of the traveller; the lock of your own hair to represent your thoughts and your true self; a silver charm (formerly a sixpence) sacred to the moon, for luck; and the sprig of rosemary, token of love and sacred to sea-spells. ❧ Ask the moon to seek for you the one best qualified to appreciate your wise mind and loving heart and, when she has found him, to send him on his journey to find you. Now write your name on paper and wrap it into a scroll with the red cord, then seal with the wax and show it to the moon and the sea. Sip wine from the flask and toast the moon, mistress of the sea, our emotional tides, and the night-time companion of us all. Take the air, sea and sky into your mind, try to become one with them, and watch the tide lapping onto the shore, seeing it bringing your beloved right to your feet. ❧ Now whisper nine times: *'Shine your light across the ocean, Guide to me my love's devotion, He who's known another life, May now make of me his wife.'* Whilst you are chanting cast the scroll into the water, but before you lose sight of it, hold up your mirror up to the moon to catch her light and then to the ocean so that it glimpses your scroll in its glass. Take the shell, rosemary and lock of your hair, and in the other hand offer the silver token up to the moon, inviting her blessing. Make a small hole in the sand or pebbles beside the water with your hand and place herb, hair and shell into it. Splash a drop of wine into the hole, cover it again, and lay your head on top of the mound for just a moment. Now you have asked the earth, too, to help. ❧ Your magic is complete at the seashore. When you return home, hold the silver up to the moon again to bring your magic into your dwelling place and stand a broom in any corner of your home. For a month, show the silver to the moon each night and sleep with it under your pillow. ❧ Within one to three months, your 'foreigner' should have appeared.

Floating down the stream ♦ To attract love closer to home. This is

an old English spell and is easier than the seashore spell if you live inland, only requiring a stream or river.

You will need

A large bunch of fresh marjoram; red ribbon; some windings of your hair from a brush or comb;

a piece of paper with your name written on it

♦ Gather or buy your marjoram on a Friday morning during the first seven days of any moon and tie it with some red ribbon. At the end of the day, untie the herb, divide it into smaller bunches, tie them with red ribbon or cotton and place them in every room of your house or apartment, keeping back one good sprig. That evening, around 6.00 p.m. if possible, carry this sprig, secured with some windings of your hair and fastened to the paper with your name on it, to a stream or river. Simply kiss the herb, offer it to the moon, ask that she find you your partner of 'true mind', and cast it swiftly into the running water. ♦ Within a month you should have had some offers.

A spell to disenchant an unwanted lover

♦ The waning moon is the time to work spells which rid you of things you no longer need or do not want around you, certainly the case in this instance.

You will need

His name written on a piece of paper; a daffodil bulb; camphor oil and leaves

♦ Plant the piece of paper with his name on it, then the daffodil, symbol of rebuttal, in a pot or in the ground. As you work, tell the plant firmly that you cannot return his affections, but you wish him well with another lover. Tell the plant each day, and on the seventh day, invite him to join you (plus a girlfriend to protect you!) for tea. Burn pungent camphor in your home all day and make sure he can still smell it at teatime. The opposite of an aphrodisiac, this should thoroughly disenchant him. Keep tending your daffodil until it blooms, when all danger will pass, and each time you meet wear some camphor oil.

A Friday night candle spell

FRIDAY NIGHTS HAVE LONG BEEN SACRED TO THE RITUALS OF LOVE – not just as an appropriate night for a working girl's date, but because the day is sacred to Venus, goddess of love. If your Friday nights have been bereft of dates lately, set aside the next one that falls on a waxing moon to do this spell.

YOU WILL NEED

A white dinner candle anointed with coriander oil (see page 118); a painting or drawing of your ideal partner (but not a photo of a film star such as Mel Gibson); a willow twig fashioned into a love knot

ON A FRIDAY NIGHT BETWEEN THE HOURS OF 6.00 AND 7.00 P.M. START YOUR SPELL. You should have made some kind of representation of your ideal mate, your own work, drawn either figuratively or as a proper sketch or watercolour. If you're not great at art, just draw a figure with perhaps one or two features you're often attracted to, such as longish hair, a beard, warm eyes or strong shoulders. As you start your magic you should roll the candle once gently in the picture, and then unwind it.

PLACE THE CANDLE IN ITS SPECIAL HOLDER (SEE INTRODUCTION) AND PUT THE DRAWING IN FRONT OF IT ON THE TABLE. Take the love knot in your right hand and light the candle with the same hand, asking Venus for her special blessing on your work. From now on you must concentrate almost hypnotically on the candle flame, feeling its power and warmth, asking that it draw love into your life. Glance at the picture you have made, and imagine someone close to you who is laughing with you and sharing a happy moment. See if you can almost feel them in the room with you. LET THE CANDLE BURN DOWN LOW, AS CLOSE TO THE BOTTOM AS YOU CAN SAFELY GO; THIS SHOULD TAKE SEVERAL HOURS. Every so often, perhaps every half hour, go back to the candle and look again into the flame, seeing yourself happy and laughing with someone you care for. Keep the love knot with you throughout the spell – a pocket would be a good place – and leave it knotted all the next day. Twenty-four hours after you began your spell, unknot the willow to free the spell (you can knot it again for another spell, another day).

IF YOUR POWERS OF CONCENTRATION ARE GOOD AND YOU HAVE GENERATED A LOT OF ENERGY AND PASSION IN YOUR THOUGHTS, a new love could have been introduced to you before the Friday one moon from the date of your spell (i.e within one month).

Nos amoureux, assis par terre
Commencèrent à deviser,
Entre le rire et le baiser,
D'un bon dîner qu'ils ve...aient
En ce lieu même, à le... loisir.
La place leur deven... chère,
Il leur fallait y rev...ir.
Tout ... sou... la verdure,
... aventure,
...buisson.
...arçon
...ore;
...anger,

Sans adieu;
Tremblante
Croyant qu...
Dans quel...
Et le serr...
Non plus...
Qu'eût-e...
Habitué...
Garden...
Leur u...
Mais la
Déjà
POÉSIES

Pensées de moi ♥ FOR THOSE WHO HAVE BEEN DISAPPOINTED IN LOVE. If yours is a story

of always attracting the wrong person and your heart has been broken once too often, this spell is for you. It will heal the wounds of past mistakes and prepare the ground for a new beginning in your love life.

YOU WILL NEED

Pansy seeds; a small terracotta pot or window box; earth and a small trowel; paper with your name written on it; some of your nail filings

♥ THE PANSY (OR HEART'S-EASE) HAS LONG BEEN THE FAVOURITE OF THOSE WHOSE HEARTS NEED HEALING. Eros is said to have released his arrow and, where it fell, the pretty-faced flower sprang up in bright colours. Grow yours to put sorrow behind you and prepare for a happier future. ♥ THIS SPELL IS BEST PERFORMED ON VALENTINE'S DAY (FEBRUARY 14), MAY DAY (MAY 1), MIDSUMMER DAY (JUNE 21), OR LAMMAS (AUGUST 1). Plant your seeds lovingly on one of the days mentioned, first putting the piece of paper with your name on it into the earth. Water in the seeds and scatter your nail filings on top. Tend your plant with care and, when the first flower blooms, pick it on a waning moon and press it in a favourite book of love poetry. Keep it with you always to attract love. ♥ CHOOSE A MAINLY YELLOW FLOWER IF YOU WANT AN INTELLECTUAL MATCH, RICH PURPLE IF YOU SEEK PASSION, OR SOFT BLUE IF YOU LONG FOR A LOVE THAT IS SIMPLE YET TRUE.

Divine intervention ❧ BY READING THE SIGNS OF THE FATES YOU MAY DISCOVER

YOUR LIFE PARTNER. ❧ At first light on Easter Sunday, visit the well at Cerne Abbas, in Dorset, or another ancient spring, to catch a glimpse of your future wife or husband reflected in the water. ❧ BRUSH YOUR HAIR IN FRONT OF A MIRROR ON ST AGNES' EVE (JANUARY 19), VALENTINE'S DAY OR HALLOWE'EN, and you will see the face of your future partner mysteriously reflected in the glass. ❧ PLACE A HAZELNUT OR APPLE PIP IN THE EMBERS OF THE FIRE ON HALLOWE'EN OR AT YULE (DECEMBER 21/22) AND SAY THE WORDS: *'If you love me pop and fly; if not, lie still and die'*. If the lover that you have in mind as you say this is the one for you, the nut will pop in the fire; if not, it will stay mute. ❧ PLACE ALL THE LETTERS OF THE ALPHABET ON INDIVIDUAL PIECES OF PAPER FACE DOWNWARDS IN A BASIN OF WATER BEFORE YOU GO TO BED ON MIDSUMMER'S EVE. The letter which turns over during the night will be the initial of your true love/wife/husband. ❧ IF YOU HAVE SOMEONE IN YOUR HEART, CARVE THEIR INITIALS INTO A LEAF AND PLACE IT IN YOUR SHOE OVERNIGHT. In the morning, if the initials are clearer they'll marry you, if not, they won't. ❧ PEEL AN APPLE IN ONE UNBROKEN PIECE AND THROW IT OVER YOUR SHOULDER; it will fall in the shape of the first letter of your intended's name. ❧ IF THREE UNMARRIED PEOPLE WITH THE SAME NAME SIT AT A TABLE AND ALL SAY *'White Horses'*, one of them will be married within the year. ❧ SEW A PIECE OF YARROW INTO A FLANNEL POUCH AND PLACE IT UNDER YOUR PILLOW. Say the words: *'Thou pretty herb of Venus' tree, Thy certain name is yarrow; Now who my lifelong partner be, Pray tell thou me tomorrow'* and your dream will reveal your true love. ❧ IF YOU WISH FOR A LOVE WITH A NUTMEG IN YOUR PALM OR POCKET, he or she will be older than you. ❧ THE FIRST NEW MOON OF THE NEW YEAR, VIEWED THROUGH A HANDKERCHIEF, will reveal the number of years you will have to wait before marriage. ❧ STIR A FIRE WITH A POKER; if it burns bright on repetition of your lover's name, the love affair will grow. ❧ BEFORE BED, ASK: *'New moon, new moon, hail to thee; this night may I my true love see'*, walk backwards to bed, watching the moon all the while, and the name or a picture of your future love will be seen in a dream. ❧ SCATTER FLOUR OR TALC UNDER A ROSEMARY BUSH ON MAY DAY OR HALLOWE'EN AND LOOK FOR THE INITIALS OF YOUR FUTURE LOVE TRACED IN IT.

FANNING
THE FLAMES

A COLLECTION OF SPELLS TO MAKE HIM YOURS. Now you have identified, and been noticed by your would-be lover; but you want to move things on – to accelerate the passion. Or, perhaps yours is a relationship of long-standing, and the physical side of the relationship has lost its spontaneity and drive. Perhaps you've been moving contentedly along for years, but there's still no sound of wedding bells. Come now to the kitchen, learn to mix a love potion or two and put the champagne bubbles back into your love life.

The ribbon of love

To BEWITCH HIM WITH THOUGHTS OF ONLY YOU. You have become practised now in the force of thought required to work your magic, so you should be quite adept enough to try this excellent little spell.

YOU WILL NEED

1 metre of red ribbon

DURING THE DAY, AS MANY TIMES AS YOU CAN FIND A SPARE FIVE OR TEN MINUTES, GO TO A QUIET SPOT AND WRAP THE LENGTH OF RIBBON AROUND YOUR RIGHT INDEX FINGER. Put it to your 'third eye' (in the centre of yur forehead between your eyebrows) and concentrate on your love with all your might: vividly imagine the smell, touch and feel of every part of his body, from the tip of his toe to the top of his head (lingering on his lips as you go). Mischievously ask him to think of you, and try to hold the image and thought for five minutes – harder than you think. Repeat several times during the day, and over the course of at least a week. *Whenever possible, sleep with the red cord under your shared pillow.*

Three woven ribbons to strengthen the bond

THIS SPELL IS BEST PERFORMED ON ST AGNES EVE (JANUARY 19) OR VALENTINE'S EVE (FEBRUARY 13).

YOU WILL NEED

3 ribbons, each 38 cm long: 1 pink, 1 lavender and 1 white; a vanilla pod

TIE THE THREE RIBBONS TOGETHER BY A KNOT IN THE TOP, SAYING YOUR PARTNER'S NAME, YOUR NAME, AND ASKING THE HELP OF VENUS OR ISIS. Speaking the three names as you go, make the ribbons into a beautiful braid and secure the end with another knot. Place the ribbons to your heart and wish your loved one 'only good'. Now wind the braid gently but firmly around the vanilla pod. THIS LOVE CHARM IS SPECIAL FOR YOU AND YOUR PARTNER; YOU SHOULD KEEP IT WITH YOU, ESPECIALLY WHEN YOU MEET EACH OTHER, AND SLEEP ON IT AT NIGHT. If you are right for each other, he will soon declare himself.

Love potions

LOVE POTIONS HAVE A SPECIAL PLACE IN OUR IMAGINATIONS, IF ONLY BECAUSE THEY SOUND SO MAGICAL AND ALLURING. They are simply a mixture of strong wines with carefully chosen herbs which will alter the state of awareness of the person partaking of them. Get into the kitchen and discover the art.

Carnations and bubbles

IN ITALY, CARNATIONS ARE A SYMBOL OF POWERFUL LOVE AND, ADDED TO WINES, WERE LONG BELIEVED TO HAVE AN APHRODISIAC PROPERTY. Borage, likewise, has an age-old reputation for bringing 'courage to the heart' and cheering the senses. It is a powerful herb indeed.

YOU WILL NEED

Petals from 9 deep red carnations; 2-3 borage leaves and as many flowers; a bottle of champagne or sparkling wine

MIX THE PETALS AND LEAVES INTO THE CHAMPAGNE AND LEAVE TO INFUSE IN THE FRIDGE FOR SEVERAL HOURS. To preserve the fizz, suspend a silver spoon in the neck of the bottle. Strain into two glasses and serve to your loved one.

THIS SHOULD PUT YOU BOTH IN THE MOOD FOR LOVE QUITE QUICKLY, FOR CHAMPAGNE ENTERS THE BLOODSTREAM QUICKER THAN OTHER WINES.

Scents of the east

THIS IS A GOOD WINTER ALTERNATIVE TO THE MORE SUMMERY POTION ABOVE; IN REALLY COLD CLIMATES THE WINE CAN BE MULLED. Jasmine is said to attract a very spiritual love, so you may move your relationship onto an altogether higher plane.

YOU WILL NEED

A vanilla pod; 1 tablespoon fresh or dried jasmine flowers; pinch cloves and cinnamon; a bottle of red wine; jasmine oil (optional)

MIX TOGETHER ALL THE INGREDIENTS APART FROM THE WINE AND OIL, AND ALLOW THEM TO STEEP FOR 30 MINUTES IN A LITTLE BOILING WATER. Add to the red wine, stirring gently, and serve, without straining, into two goblets.

IF YOU DAB A LITTLE JASMINE OIL AT YOUR THROAT AND SIP THIS WITH YOUR PARTNER, you should soon find yourselves completely absorbed in one another.

Aphrodite's oil or 'Cupid's tears' ♥ A CURE FOR THE WANING

LIBIDO. This variation on the love potion is a blend of oils you make up to create your own original perfume. It works better than a wonderbra to grab his (and everyone else's) attention and should be a cure for your or your partner's waning libido. ♥ ON A FRIDAY NIGHT CLOSE TO A FULL MOON, WHEN IT IS AT ITS MAXIMUM POTENCY, blend your own scent by choosing your favourite three of the following aphrodisiac oils: into 25ml of almond oil, add up to 10 drops (your choice of proportion) oil of lavender, rose geranium, ylang ylang, tuberose (expensive but very powerful), gardenia or jasmine. Add 1 drop of musk oil at the end. Wear between your breasts and behind your knees and watch for the extraordinary effect it will have on your partner.

A sensual massage oil ♥ To TURN YOUR PARTNER ON. Instead of, or as well as, the

personal scent described above, try mixing up this 'scentsational' massage oil. If you feel it's too early in your budding relationship to suggest a massage, choose a sunny day and offer to apply some suntan oil, in which case you will need to mix the following ingredients with some protective sunscreen.

YOU WILL NEED

2 drops of real musk oil (not cheap but a good investment) and 8 drops of frangipani oil (or peony if you can't find frangipani), diluted in 20 ml peach kernel oil (or suntan lotion)

♥ MASSAGE IN THE OIL USING LARGE SWEEPING CIRCULAR MOVEMENTS, CONCENTRATING ON THE AREA AROUND THE BASE OF THE SPINE, AND WAIT FOR THE EFFECT.

The lavender candle ❧

To make him burn with desire. Years ago, when I had a relationship with an older man whose interest in sex was limited, I lived on the following spell week after week to keep the passion going. Ultimately it could not change the fact that we were not destined to be life-partners, but we had a lot more fun in the interim than we otherwise might have had. You need to perform this spell over seven nights, at the same time each night.

YOU WILL NEED

A lavender-scented dinner candle (from a specialist supplier or anoint your own lavender-coloured candle with lavender essential oil, see page 118); 7 small pieces of paper with your name written on each one

❧ BEGIN THIS SPELL, PREFERABLY ON A WAXING MOON, ON ANY NIGHT OF THE WEEK, OR EARLY IN THE MORNING IF THIS IS A TIME YOU CAN RELIABLY BE PRIVATE ON SEVEN CONSECUTIVE DAYS. Make six notches along the length of the candle to make seven equal intervals. Place it in your special holder and say your lover's name seven times. Now take the first piece of paper, fold it in half and light it with a match. Quickly carry it to the wick and light your candle from the name, leaving it resting in the wick if possible. ❧ AS YOU DO THIS, SAY YOUR CHANT: *'Flame burn bright through the night, Let me give you real delight',* and see your lover's face glowing in the flame. You must now wait patiently for the flame to burn down to the first notch, at which point you should use your moistened fingers to extinguish it. ❧ EACH NIGHT OR MORNING, AT EXACTLY THE SAME TIME, REPEAT THE PROCESS UNTIL YOU HAVE BURNT THE CANDLE TO THE END. On the next night, or sometimes during the seven-night process, he will come calling on you with a deep longing.

To create a sensual ambience ❧

ON THE SUBJECT OF SCENT USED TO AROUSE PASSIONS, use lavender oil mixed with rose petals, orris root, rose and patchouli oils in one of the following three ways: ❧ BURN ALL THE INGREDIENTS TOGETHER ON A CHARCOAL BURNER OR IN A ROOM FRAGRANCER TO CREATE AN ATMOSPHERE OF LOVE BEFORE A DATE. ❧ MIX THEM WITH BACHELOR'S BUTTON AND MYRTLE LEAVES AND SEW THEM INTO A RED OR PURPLE SACHET TO CARRY WITH YOU AT ALL TIMES. ❧ USE THEM TO FORM THE BASIS OF A POTPOURRI, ADDED TO 1 CUP FRESH OR DRIED VERVAIN LEAVES, AND PLACE IT BY THE DOOR OF YOUR BEDROOM. Each time you enter the room, stir the potpourri with the ring finger of your left hand (the vein is said to lead straight to the heart) and love will flourish there!

A moonlight spell
To take control of his on/off affection. Perhaps your relationship is in difficulty because you're not certain your partner is really sincere with you: his affections, attentions and passions may be very on/off. A close friend might advise you to ditch it and find a new love, but if you want to give it one last chance to see if it could ever be the real thing, this might help. You must be prepared to find out whether your love is going to last through this, the test of truth of intent. Once you have asked the moon goddess to illuminate your lover's hidden thoughts the relationship will begin to falter if it is better that it should end: you alone can decide.

You will need

A small rosemary seedling; a small vervain seedling; 9 flowers (preferably roses or carnations); carnation oil

Perform this spell on a Monday, the day of the moon, when it is nearly but not yet past full. In a large pot, window box or herb bed, plant your rosemary and vervain plantlets together, not so close that they strangle each other nor so far apart that they lose touch. Around the plants, place the nine flowers in a kind of clock face. Speak to the moon and ask for help and honesty in your undertaking. Touch each flower lightly and say your lover's name and, when you have touched the ninth (the number of completion), ask your love to put away his indifferent habits if he really cares for you and to love you more completely. **Now you must say the words:** *'Carnation (or rose) one, our spell's begun. Carnation two, to me be true. Carnation three, be drawn to me. Carnation four, knock at my door. Carnation five, come share my life. Carnation six, our souls shall mix. Carnation seven, blessed now by heaven. Carnation eight, are you my mate? Carnation nine, no more repine. Nine love flowers beside me lay, bid my love the truth to say.'* **Let the flowers wither over several days, then crumble them into a dish.** Add a few drops of carnation oil and let them smoulder in the ashes of a fire or on a stove to release the most powerful aroma. During the burning, ask again to be told the direction of your love relationship. **Within nine months, either your partner will commit himself to you properly, or you will separate so a new, true love can find you.**

A love charm to make him yours

YOU'VE BEEN TOGETHER FOR SOME TIME NOW AND YOU KNOW THIS IS THE PARTNER FOR YOU. Perhaps because he's male, or because he's been hurt in love before, or even because he wants to buy you a house before he pops any questions, the subject of marriage seems to be taboo. There is no point in trying this spell if the partner you have in mind is spoken for elsewhere or is ultimately wrong for you; but if you feel he just needs a push to make up his mind, this spell is tailor-made for the purpose.

YOU WILL NEED

Orange blossom, rose buds or apple blossom; 1 pink or white candle; neroli or orange blossom oil;
a willow twig; a strand or lock of your lover's hair

TO BEGIN THIS SPELL YOU MUST MAKE A 'LOVE ALTAR'; THIS WILL BE GOOD FOR ALL LOVE SPELLS, IN FACT, BUT CRUCIAL TO THIS ONE. Lay a rose–pink cloth or silken scarf over a small table and decorate it with orange blossom, rose buds or apple blossom. Many cultures consider orange blossom sacred to weddings; the scent is passionate and yet soothing. CHOOSE A FRIDAY AND A WAXING MOON TO WORK THE SPELL. Light a pink candle, or white if you prefer, and ask divine blessing on your workings. Address your thoughts either to Venus/Isis or Eros/Cupid. Anoint yourself with a few neat drops of neroli or orange blossom oil (diluted in a few drops of sweet almond oil if your skin is sensitive to it neat). Now take your willow twig and weave it into a knot with your lover's hair, saying all the while: *'Declare yourself to me truly (first name); I mean you no harm and can contribute to our life of settled joy!'* Place the knot beside the flowers on the love altar, and ask for divine guidance and help.

YOU MUST KEEP THE KNOT WITH YOU WHEN YOU SEE YOUR LOVE AND ALWAYS WEAR THE ORANGE BLOSSOM OIL, A SIGNAL THAT YOU ARE READY TO COMMIT TO YOUR RELATIONSHIP. At least once a week, add a few drops of the oil to your bath in a cleansing, loving ritual. Before long (if he's the right one for you) you'll have subtly worn down his resistance.

HEALING
THE BREACH

SPELLS TO SEE YOU THROUGH THE UPS AND DOWNS OF YOUR RELATIONSHIPS. Even the best planned and most lovingly tended relationships have periods when they go through rocky patches. These may be caused by misunderstandings or a failure to say what you really mean, when the potential longevity of a promising relationship could be jeopardised by the smallest snag, such as a stubborn quarrel or a protracted silence. In this chapter, then, a little enchantment helps you to soothe arguments and heal impasses. This is a tale of reconciliation.

The ribbon of love no. 2 ♥ MAKING CONTACT. This spell is intended for those

who are waiting for the other side to make the approach after an argument. Use it if you're not sure where your lover is, or if you know he's just being reticent, or even as a preamble to making the telephone call yourself and being sure of a fair hearing. But beware, it won't work if you're the guilty party and, having misbehaved or thrown a tantrum, you owe your partner an apology.

YOU WILL NEED

1 metre of red ribbon

♥ PERFORM THIS SPELL ON ANY MOON OR DAY OF THE WEEK, but if the quarrel has been fierce and you need extra strength, use the full moon. You must also bring a calm mind to the task, since tearful outbursts and hot emotion will send confused signals to your partner and could cause fears of renewed hostility. ♥ WRAP THE RIBBON AROUND THE INDEX FINGER OF YOUR RIGHT HAND AND PLACE IT ON YOUR 'THIRD EYE' (BETWEEN YOUR BROWS). Start thinking intently of your loved one; when you have a clear and powerful sense of his closeness, use the ribbon on your forehead to 'talk' to him and tell him you're sorry about the upset and would love to speak to him. Urge him to contact you. ♥ TRY TO HOLD THIS CONCENTRATION FOR A FEW MINUTES WITHOUT LETTING YOUR MIND WANDER, THEN REST, SENDING HIM LOVING THOUGHTS BEFORE YOU BREAK OFF. Pick up the ribbon again in an hour and repeat the process, several times in the day/evening if possible. He will soon be straining to contact you: but when the call comes, don't be distant. Remember to meet him half way.

Frozen honey ♥

To SWEETEN HIM UP. This is another excellent spell for improving relations after a fight. It is also a good choice if relations have been souring between you for a little while and you want to sweeten things up again.

YOU WILL NEED

FOR THE CLEANSING BATH: *Salt; valerian root, rosemary and rue (though be careful with this last if you have sensitive skin as you may react to the contact; handle it on a cloudy day); rose oil*

FOR THE SPELL: *2 small pieces of paper with your and your partner's names written, one on each; a tiny plastic pot or container; some vervain leaves; a small pot of clover honey; a freezer*

♥ IF YOU REALLY WANT TO PUT YOUR HEART AND SOUL INTO THIS SPELL YOU SHOULD BEGIN BY RUNNING YOURSELF A CLEANSING BATH BEFORE YOU DO IT. This is a warm bath to which is added a spoonful of salt along with some crushed valerian root, rosemary and rue. Take your thoughts of love with you into the bath and, with an honest heart, speak out loud your reasons for choosing to perform the honey spell. Make sure you are really motivated by love and not by a wish to bind your love to you. After your bath, rub your hands with a little lotion to which you have added a few drops of rose oil. ♥ NOW YOU ARE READY TO PERFORM THE SPELL: Place the two pieces of paper with your names written on together, so that the names face in to each other, and place them at the bottom of your container. Put a few vervain leaves on top. Now take the honey and pour it into the container so that it generously covers the contents. Make a vow of warmth and affection to your love, and say: *'Sweeten ye up, in this healing cup'*. Pass your hands over the top three times in a caressing gesture, then imagine a honey-coloured glow bathing you and your love as you stand together, holding hands. finally, place the container in a space in your freezer where it will not be disturbed. ♥ WITHIN A FEW DAYS YOU SHOULD DETECT A DEFINITE IMPROVEMENT IN THE RELATIONSHIP.

'May this rift know short shrift' ♥ TO GIVE A BREAK-UP A CHANCE OF

HEALING. Comfrey has long been the favourite herb for mending breaks – quite literally, for it was traditionally fashioned into a poultice and applied to broken bones to heal them. It is used in protection spells as well as healing spells, but this ritual calls on its powers of reuniting, to bring together two people who have grown apart.

YOU WILL NEED

2 passport-sized photos: one each of you and your lover; 2 or 3 comfrey flowers with leaves; a length of white ribbon;
a steaming bowl or cauldron of boiling water to which you have added a few drops of spearmint oil; a small lidded box

♥ CLEANSE YOUR SPELL-WORKING AREA FIRST, NOT ONLY WITH YOUR BROOM OR VACUUM CLEANER, BUT ALSO WITH A BEAM OF WHITE LIGHT SENT AROUND THE ROOM FROM YOUR MIND'S EYE. This will neutralise any existing bad feeling between you and your beloved. ♥ TAKE THE PHOTOS, FACING TOWARDS EACH OTHER, AND SANDWICH THE COMFREY IN BETWEEN THEM. Wrap the white ribbon gently around them and secure with a bow, chanting softly all the while: *'May this rift, know short shrift'.* Put your hands together in a prayer position with the photo package between your palms, asking for help in healing the enmity between you. Then pass the package through the steam of purification coming from your kettle or cauldron. ♥ THE SPELL IS COMPLETED BY PLACING THE PHOTO PACKAGE IN THE LITTLE BOX AND PLACING IT SOMEWHERE HIGH IN YOUR HOME, PREFERABLY FACING EAST. Leave it until the argument is mended, then open the box and free the photos with a word of thanks.

A loving cup ☙ MAKE THIS LOVE POTION TO SIP WITH YOUR PARTNER AT YOUR FIRST MEETING

TOGETHER AFTER A RIFT. Blend your brew in advance and allow it to steep for several days in a cool cupboard.

YOU WILL NEED

1 teaspoon apothecary's rose (petals); a few leaves of alecost (or costmary); a pinch of saffron; a bottle of sherry

☙ CRUSH THE HERBS AND FLOWERS TOGETHER (THE COSTMARY INTENSIFIES THE SCENT OF THE ROSES AND SAFFRON) AND ADD TO THE BOTTLE OF SHERRY. Store in a cool place for a few days; when you wish to serve it to your partner, strain into small glasses. This lovely concoction will ease the tensions at what otherwise might be a tricky meeting.

The red rose and the briar ☙ TO MAKE YOUR RELATIONSHIP CLOSER.

If you feel you are growing apart from someone you love and want to rediscover that special feeling of closeness, try growing two plants into a lover's embrace.

YOU WILL NEED

2 pieces of paper; 2 creeping or climbing plants, traditionally a red rose and a briar rose, but ivy, honeysuckle, jasmine, wisteria or clematis would have the same effect

☙ WRITE YOUR NAME AND THAT OF YOUR BELOVED ON TWO PIECES OF PAPER. Take your two healthy plants and plant them, each with one of the pieces of paper buried beneath its roots, on either side of a low wall or fence. As they grow they can reach out to one another, eventually forming a strong lover's knot. Water the plants to get them established and make a vow to be true to your other half. Each time you water, train them towards each other a little. ☙ AFTER ONE GOOD SUMMER'S GROWTH YOU SHOULD SEE SOME PROGRESS, BOTH IN THE GARDEN AND IN THE RELATIONSHIP.

Burying your differences ♥ To put the past behind you. If your relationship

has undergone a truly trying time but you are now on the mend together – reunited perhaps after a serious break but still on uncertain ground – the following short but highly symbolic spell may help you both to go forward with clear hearts.

You will need

Objects chosen to represent your 'bundle of sorrows' from the past (such as scissors or a knife to symbolise sharp words,

a blank page to symbolise lack of communication, your business card to represent preoccupation with work,

a green marble 'eye' for jealousy, a hammer for physical blows, a broken watch for wasted time etc);

a young rose or geranium plant (choose the latter if you need to put it in a pot)

♥ In this ritual you simply work together, or alone if need be, to turn over a new leaf and bury your sorrows deep in the ground, never more to rise. Choose an early morning, soon after sunrise, and work positively and with complete faith. ♥ Over the top of the objects you have chosen, plant your young plant, in pot or ground, in order to create something beautiful and strong out of your past mistakes. As you bury the objects, make a pledge to learn from your mistakes. ♥ Water your plant together whenever possible.

A friend was very successful in restoring her love affair with this spell, and it had interesting side effects in her garden. She chose a hydrangea for her plant, and placed a collection of copper cooking pans and a whole canteen of cutlery under it, because in the past they had always argued at meal times. Over the next few months her love affair grew strong again and her hydrangea turned blue – the only one in a collection of pink hydrangeas. The scientific reason for this was the addition of metal to the soil, but she felt that the plant had got the blues instead of her!

The candle of truth ❦ To KNOW IF SOMEONE IS DECEIVING YOU. Sometimes you may

feel you can put the past behind you only if you know the absolute truth about what has happened to cause the rift; then you can forgive and heal. Be sure you really want to know what your loved one has to say before you do this, the truth spell.

YOU WILL NEED

A mirror; a white candle; incense of narcissus oil to relax your partner; a vase of geraniums, or primroses; a glass of wine

❦ THIS SPELL SHOULD BE PERFORMED ONLY ON THE 7TH OF THE MONTH. Invite your love to sit in front of a mirror with the offer of a neck and shoulder massage. In front of you light the white candle and burn the oil – very relaxing. You should also have the flowers, all symbols of doubt until better acquaintance, in front of the mirror. ❦ AS YOU WORK YOUR HANDS, SPEAK SOFTLY AND HYPNOTICALLY SO YOUR LOVE RELAXES COMPLETELY AND, WHEN YOU FEEL THE MOMENT IS RIGHT, ASK THREE QUESTIONS. Ask the reflection of your lover's face and make sure he answers the reflection of yours. The first two questions should not be too serious, rather light-hearted in fact. They could relate to your love's plans for the week at work, or about his family. Notice his expression as he answers. Finally, ask him the question to which you want to know the truthful answer: if he answers honestly, you will know from his face in the mirror – for, though he may be able to fib a little to others, he cannot lie to himself. You will know!

Three's a crowd

THERE ARE TWO SPELLS YOU MIGHT CONSIDER IF THE PROBLEMS YOU FACE ARE BECAUSE OF A THIRD PARTY. In a bona fide situation, where your partner is being wooed away by the 'unscrupulous mistress' figure, I think it is perfectly correct to put your own fighting energies out into the cosmos and ask the gods to favour you with victory. However, be warned: you may be able to fool yourself about your motives, but if you are trying to bind a person to you against their will, and putting a negative vibration onto someone else in the process, you will get this back in threefold measure. It is not worth the consequences, so unless your heart and motives are completely fair, leave these spells alone.

The mad tea party

A SPELL TO TEST THE STRENGTH OF HIS AFFECTION.

YOU WILL NEED

A cup of tea or coffee; your nail filings

MAKE HIM A CUP OF COFFEE OR TEA AND PUT SOME OF YOUR NAIL FILINGS INTO HIS CUP, TO REMIND HIM OF THE ESSENCE OF YOU. This is a powerful spell for the properly motivated: my mother swore by it for protecting her relationship.

Freezing off a rival

A SPELL TO DETER A THIRD PARTY.

YOU WILL NEED

A small piece of paper with the name of your rival written on it; a tiny envelope; sealing wax;
a small plastic container; spring water

PERFORM THIS SPELL ON A WANING MOON, NOT FAR PAST FULL. Pop the piece of paper into a tiny envelope (gift card size), then seal it with sealing wax. As you do this, say over and over that you mean the person (address them by name) no harm and wish them absolute luck in love with someone else, but not with your partner. Send them warm feelings and ask that they retreat from their pursual of your beloved. Now place the envelope into the container, and top with spring water, saying again *'I mean you no harm, but spare my love your charm'*. Place the container in the freezer and ask a blessing on your magic. If this is merely an interloper, and not in fact your lover's real soul-mate in your stead, the powers of her attraction will steadily wane. BE CONFIDENT AND DO NOT RESORT TO SNIDE REMARKS IN THE MEANTIME.

FAMILY MATTERS

4

Fertility spells and protection for the family. The best work done today to help women who find it difficult to conceive is in fertility clinics, where miracles actually seem to happen on a regular basis. But for many women the problems are not so severe and a little help from the magical, natural world will be enough to get things moving. In this chapter, I can make no promises but I can say truthfully that many, many satisfied friends and clients are living proof that a little magic can be a big help in the mysterious business of procreation. All fertility spells should be worked on a waxing moon.

The parsley diet ❧ To aid conception. The ingredients in this spell have a long connection of use in aiding fertility and are excellent for female hormones.

You will need

Fresh flat-leafed parsley; cucumbers; lettuce; fennel bulb; sunflower seeds; pine nuts, hazelnuts and walnuts; fresh basil leaves

❧ From the moment you decide you wish to become pregnant, include these ingredients in a daily salad, together with whatever other ingredients you fancy. At the same time, start growing some parsley in your garden or on your windowsill, and pat the earth around it each day asking for the blessing of Mother Earth. This can be a very effective ritual for some.

Oak and mistletoe: the royal marriage ❧ You may wish to do one of these rather more symbolic rituals at the same time as your diet. Oak, and the mistletoe that grew in its branches, were sacred above all else to the Druids, who knew their powers. The acorn is a strong talisman of fertility and increased sexual powers; some say it can even cure impotence. ❧ Find two acorns and pour a few drops of ale or wine over the roots of the oak tree from which they have fallen to thank it for its blessing. Bless the acorns under a full moon, and recharge them every month. Give your partner one acorn to carry and carry the other yourself. ❧ Mistletoe, of course, presides over Yule-time kisses, wondering whom to favour with its blessings of fertility. You could simply carry a piece whilst you're wishing to conceive. ❧ Take an oak bath (see page 106) before making love when you're trying to conceive. ❧ Finally, you can make a fertility altar, dressed in fresh green flowers and with a green candle which you should burn to seek the blessings of nature. Pray each day to the female divinity and ask to be allowed to share in the powers of creation.

Three for a girl

A SURE SPELL FOR A GIRL BABY. The desire to choose the sex of your child is hardly new. The inheritance of property and power of the family often depended on giving birth to 'heirs male', but daughters had their place too. Not only important for ensuring marriage contracts (neighbouring conflicts were sorted out more easily through marriage than war), daughters were a guarantee that any future offspring were unquestionably of your own family line. If, like me, you would love to have a daughter, or if there are already boys in the family and you're longing for a little balance, this spell will give you an excellent chance of making a girl. Of course, you have to begin before you're pregnant.

YOU WILL NEED

FOR EACH NIGHT: *3 pink dinner candles; lemon and lime essential oils; 3 flowers, preferably pinks; half a cup of freshly squeezed lemon juice; a douche*

BEFORE YOU BEGIN YOU SHOULD SPEND AT LEAST A WEEK, PRIOR TO OVULATION, EATING A DIET OF ACID-RICH FOODS, OR AT LEAST MAKE SURE THAT EVERY BREAKFAST IS FOLLOWED BY A GLASS OF ORANGE JUICE. It is helpful if your partner joins you in this. Work the ritual of this spell over three nights: your most fertile night and those either side of it. On the evenings you have set aside, group the three candles closely together and light them, saying: *'The first candle was loneliness, The second we both share, The third is for our daughter, For whom we now prepare'.* Run yourself a warm, but not hot, bath to share with your partner and add a capful of each essential oil. AFTER A SHORT RELAXING BATH, PLACE THE THREE FLOWERS IN A VASE IN FRONT OF THE CANDLES, SAYING THE WORDS OF THE SPELL AGAIN BUT REPLACING THE WORD 'CANDLE' WITH 'FLOWER'. Whilst you do this, imagine a huge beam of pink coloured light circling through the room and cleansing the environment. PRIOR TO LOVEMAKING, THE MOST IMPORTANT PART OF THE SPELL IS THE DOUCHING. It is imperative that you douche with a solution of the lemon juice and one cup of warm water and leave a little for your partner to bathe his vital parts in too – this helps attract the female sperm. Let the juice take effect for about ten minutes, during which time you should both imagine the pink light surrounding you. *'Think Pink'* during your lovemaking, and let the candles burn down in the afterglow. REPEAT THE SPELL ON THE FOLLOWING TWO NIGHTS.

Four for a boy

🐱 AN EQUALLY SURE SPELL FOR A BABY BOY. Unsurprisingly perhaps, the more frequently used version of this spell was for a little boy, the time-honoured guarantee of immortality for the family clan. This spell remained popular long after the heyday of other witchcraft – especially since, in England and many other European countries, the inheritance of property and titles was dependent on producing a male heir. I hope, though, that this spell will be your choice only if you already have girls and want to bring a male balance to the family.

YOU WILL NEED

ON EACH NIGHT: *4 blue dinner candles; dill seeds; 2-3 drops fennel oil; Epsom salts or bicarbonate of soda; 4 blue periwinkles or bluebells (a fairy flower); a douche.*

🐱 THIS SPELL FOLLOWS THE FORMAT OF THE SPELL FOR A GIRL, AND THE DIET PRIOR TO CONCEPTION IS JUST AS IMPORTANT BUT ALKALINE RATHER THAN ACID. In days past this consisted mainly of a large consumption of soda bread (an Irish favourite) as well as adding dill seeds to salads and meat dishes, partly to counteract the acid reaction to food. Drinking fennel tea is helpful, and it goes without saying that the avoidance of acidic foods (like citrus fruits) is essential. 🐱 OVER THE THREE NIGHTS WHEN YOU HAVE CALCULATED YOUR OPTIMUM FERTILITY, LIGHT YOUR FOUR BLUE CANDLES IN THE BEDROOM, AT THE SAME TIME SAYING: *'One was lonely sorrow, Two our coupled joy, Three we have our little girl, Four is for our boy'.* Now you should run your bath with some fennel oil and either Epsom salts or, best of all, a large spoonful of bicarbonate of soda. Take your bath together, relaxing and breathing in the fragrance. While you sit, cleanse the area around you from your mind with a beam of strong blue light, asking for a blessing on your magic. Retiring to the bedroom, group the candles near to the flowers and caress each blue flower, at the same time saying the same rhyme again. 🐱 SO MUCH FOR THE SPIRITUAL CONTENT OF YOUR SPELL. The vital physical piece is to douche with a mild solution of bicarbonate of soda and warm water (about two teaspoons in half a cup of water) and, crucially, to ask your partner to sprinkle some neat powder on his organ (it doesn't sting). This is very important, so if he really wants a son don't let him shrink (literally!) in embarrassment. Allow about ten minutes (no more) for the soda to work before lovemaking. 🐱 REPEAT THIS WHOLE RITUAL OVER THE FOLLOWING TWO NIGHTS.

Top 10 old wives' tales about pregnancy

'IF IT'S A GREAT YEAR FOR NUTS, IT'S A GREAT YEAR FOR CHILDREN.' 🐱 CARRY A RABBIT'S FOOT FOR FERTILITY. 🐱 DON'T CROSS YOUR LEGS WHILST PREGNANT – it hinders birth. 🐱 DON'T GET MARRIED AFTER SUNSET IF YOU WANT TO BE SURE OF HAVING CHILDREN. 🐱 STREWING NUTS, ESPECIALLY HAZELNUTS, has the longest connection with fertility for young married couples. 🐱 IF YOU ARE IN THE COMPANY OF TWO PREGNANT WOMEN AND YOU WANT TO AVOID GETTING PREGNANT, slap your backside three times. 🐱 IF ANOTHER WOMAN'S BABY LOOKS RIGHT AT YOU FROM BETWEEN ITS LEGS YOU WILL GET PREGNANT. 🐱 WEARING A COAT BELONGING TO, OR SITTING IN A CHAIR OCCUPIED BY A PREGNANT WOMAN HAS THE SAME EFFECT. 🐱 IF A MOTHER GIVES AWAY ALL THE BABY CLOTHES AND THE CRADLE THAT SHE HAS, she will be sure to have another baby (true in my case). 🐱 KISS UNDER THE MISTLETOE THEN PICK ONE OF THE BERRIES AND YOU WILL HAVE A CHILD WITHIN THE YEAR.

Protection spells ♠

TWO TREES, SACRED TO THE DRUIDS, HAVE LONG BEEN WELL-KNOWN FOR THEIR PROTECTIVE POWERS. In fact, the expression 'touch wood', to make sure your luck holds, comes from the practice of touching trees to secure the blessing of the tree spirits, which later was replaced by the idea of touching a piece of Christ's true cross. ♠ IF YOU WANT TO GIVE YOUR FAMILY AND HOME EXTRA HELP AND PROTECTION, THE FIRST STEP WOULD BE TO PLANT A ROWAN TREE — for it is asserted that anyone dwelling in a house hosting this tree shall be blessed and have special protection from fairy and angel folk. These are not large trees, so it is conceivable to grow one in a big pot. ♠ THE SECOND TREE OF PROTECTION AND, SOME SAY, ONE WITH THE POWER TO GRANT WISHES, IS THE WITCHES' FAVOURITE, THE WILLOW. This was one of the original Druid trees from the tree/moon calendar (see page 117), and the moon associated with it is sometimes called 'Willow moon, the witches' moon'. The willow has powers of love, healing and fertility, but if you want to safeguard your home, family and property, grow a willow in the garden near a stream or old well to influence the Fates.

A willow spell ♠

TO PROTECT THE FAMILY. If you're a city dweller who wishes to protect your home and family you can bring willow branches into your house or apartment and make a kind of altar for them. You can also do the following spell.

YOU WILL NEED

2 drops each rosemary, geranium and frankincense oil in about 15 ml almond oil; willow branches for cleansing; a growing cyclamen plant; a white candle

♠ CHOOSE A WAXING MOON. Burn the oils in a burner and carry it through the rooms of your home to cleanse them all. In the area of the hearth, or wherever you all sit grouped the most often, perform your spell. Lay the willow branches and the potted cyclamen (white or red is best) on a table, and light a pure white candle. With your herb oils still burning and with vivid thought, take a beam of white light from the candle in your mind's eye and spin it like a tornado around the room and around each member of the household, cleansing away all negativity. Each morning you can surround your family afresh in this protective white light.

♠ TAKE THE WILLOW BRANCHES AND WEAVE THEM INTO A SMALL WREATH, BATHE IT IN THE WHITE LIGHT, AND HANG IT ABOVE YOUR FRONT DOOR. Light a fresh white candle in the same place once a month on the new moon to recharge the positive atmosphere.

BLACK CATS
& OTHER
FAMILY
MEMBERS

HOW TO KEEP YOUR FAMILY HAPPY AND WELL-BALANCED. Even the most magically inspired lifestyle will know its share of challenges. One such, in my experience, is how to deal gently and unmenacingly with people who are pushy and interfering. It may be a neighbour, an overprotective friend or a work colleague ~ all well-meaning but unable to take the subtle hint that you don't appreciate their constant and overbearing advice. However the most difficult of all interfering relationships is with parents, yours or his.

The in-laws' tea party

A SPELL TO DEAL WITH A DIFFCULT MOTHER-IN-LAW. In this relatively straightforward ritual it is important to analyse the reasons for the strained relationship you have with your partner's family. Almost certainly, a note of jealousy over your dominant role in her son's life is the culprit; but sometimes a fear of not living up to your expectations, or a lack of knowing how to approach you, can be the real underlying problem. Ylang ylang and cypress oils both combat feelings of jealousy, ylang ylang with the added ability to counteract detachment and fear of social contact.

YOU WILL NEED

The ingredients for the Frozen Honey spell (page 45); an afternoon tea spread of sandwiches and little cakes; a pot of strong tea or coffee; your nail filings; a candle anointed with ylang ylang or cypress oil

ON A WANING MOON (BECAUSE YOU ARE DRIVING AWAY NEGATIVE FEELINGS) PERFORM THE FROZEN HONEY spell, but place your name and that of your mother-in-law (or whoever it is you wish to contact) in the container, then in the freezer as described. On the same day, invite the difficult party to tea, and make it a lavish spread to demonstrate a real effort of generosity. Also, the more food you offer, the more liquid she'll probably drink. In the cup she will use, place a few of your nail filings (if you're battling both in-laws, put them straight into the pot) and let her quietly ingest your essence. Light the candle and let the scent pervade the atmosphere before tea. Circle her with white light in your mind whilst you do this, and ask her to see that you are not an enemy. Imagine her relaxing more with you. AVOID ALL SENSITIVE SUBJECTS DURING THE ENSUING TEA PARTY, AND REPEAT THE SPELL AT INTERVALS EVERY FEW WEEKS UNTIL YOU HAVE THE PROBLEM UNDER CONTROL.

Frankincense & mirth ● A POTION TO ENABLE DIFFICULT RELATIVES TO GET ALONG.

If the days are long and sunny and a picnic or garden party seems more appropriate than an afternoon tea, you might prefer the following spell, or potion, which can be used on anyone or in any situation, such as an occasion where some of the guests don't get on with each other. Ideal for a wedding or engagement party which requires disparate elements in the family to come together for a few hours.

YOU WILL NEED

A burner with smouldering frankincense (charcoal, or oil in water); borage flowers; lemon juice; 1 teaspoon sugar; sliced strawberries; a bottle of champagne or sparkling wine

● PREPARE THE AREA WITH A QUICK CLEANSING RITUAL USING FRANKINCENSE OIL SPATTERED ON THE CLOTH WHERE YOU WILL EAT (IF ANYONE WANTS TO KNOW WHAT YOU'RE DOING YOU CAN TELL THEM, TRUTHFULLY, THAT FRANKINCENSE OIL KEEPS INSECTS AWAY), THEN BURN SOME OF THE OIL FOR THE DURATION OF THE GATHERING. Mix your drink a few hours beforehand to allow the properties of the borage to develop. Borage has a very calming effect and is said to bring about a state of forgetfulness when mixed with wine. Blend the flowers with a tablespoon of lemon juice and a teaspoon of sugar and let stand for an hour. Add the sliced strawberries and marinate for another hour: the borage will subtly alter the taste, quite deliciously. Add the champagne or sparkling wine about an hour before it is required, and cover to preserve the fizz. ● SERVE TO YOUR GUESTS, THEN STAND BACK AND WATCH AS TENSE FAMILY MEMBERS STOP FEUDING AND ALL BEGIN TO LAUGH TOGETHER.

Cutting the cord ● To make over-protective parents loosen their grip. This

procedure encourages your family to hold onto you less tightly, without losing the bond of warmth.

You will need

1 metre of red cord or ribbon; a photo of your parents; a pair of pinking shears tied with a white bow

● Working on a waning moon, take your cord or ribbon and bind it around the index finger of your right hand. Place it to your third eye and close your eyes, thinking lovingly of your parents. Take the photo of them and hold it in front of you, looking deeply at the image, whilst you send a strong mental message to them to loosen their hold on you without fear of losing your love. Now take the ribbon and cut it in half with the bow-tied shears; kiss both halves and keep them in separate drawers. ● Send them a blessing for their safety, and ask them to relax. You should notice an immediate difference.

A rosemary remedy ● To help restore your concentration. There are times when

none of the family are quite performing at their peak. Tension, stress or overtiredness can all be contributing to a general sense of malaise, so here is an excellent ritual to help get your concentration and mental energy back on track, which you will find over the years has many applications.

You will need

25 g freshly picked rosemary; rosemary oil; a base lotion or thick quality night creme, preferably unperfumed

● This draws on rosemary's ancient association with waking up the brain, a custom so strong that ancient Greek scholars wore garlands of the herb to help them think. ● If someone in the family is preparing for an exam or studying hard, prepare a tea of rosemary using flowering tops, or several sprigs if the flowers are not out, and infusing in one litre of boiling water. Leave it for five to ten minutes, strain, and drink three cupfuls through the day, sweetening with honey if desired.Before they go into their exam (or meeting), rub a mild ointment of rosemary on their temples: about two drops rosemary oil mixed with one tablespoon of good quality skin lotion. This will stimulate their senses and keep them alert. This could make all the difference.

'Child in honey, child in light' ❧ To control a stubborn child.

All the psychological strategies you can think of are often powerless against the wiles of a wilful child. They seem to embarrass us effortlessly at social occasions and sometimes prove a danger to themselves, too, as they career towards some impending catastrophe.

You will need

A small photo of your child; a jar of lavender or clover honey; sealing wax; 1 metre of white ribbon

❧ Perform this spell on a Thursday, with a waxing moon. Before you begin, spend a few minutes in your child's room soaking up the feeling of the child: breathe in their smell and their aura, and imagine you can hear their laughter. Take the best element of your child's behaviour with you in your mind, and go to your protection altar to make your spell. All the while you are working, think of your child cocooned in a spiral of white light. ❧ Place the small photo inside the jar of honey, saying: *'Child in honey, child in light, Let your cares take elfin flight; Smooth your thorns, be gone sour moods, And witness sunshine interludes. Stamp your foot no more from hence, Nor show you such indifference. Speech is silver, silence gold – Now you must do just as you're told! With love.'* Send all your love to your child, and reseal the jar. Add sealing wax around the rim, and secure with a white ribbon. Place the jar on a high shelf or cupboard, out of the way but not somewhere dark. ❧ Every so often, touch the jar and repeat the words to recharge the power of the spell.

To end conflict between siblings ❧ Here is another spell to

help with fractious children, this time brothers and/or sisters who fight. Get your children to do the spell above with a photo of each other, both placed in the honey jar together, telling them it will bring them good luck and grant a wish if they kiss afterwards and are good. You must say the incantation, but having them do the action is very effective.

To calm a relative or friend in distress

THERE COMES A TIME IF A CLOSE FRIEND OR RELATIVE IS IN SEVERE DISTRESS WHEN TEA AND SYMPATHY ARE NOT QUITE ENOUGH AND YOU REALLY NEED TO TAKE CONTROL OF A SPIRALLING SITUATION. Whether the crisis has occurred through some shock to the system (such as witnessing an accident) or perhaps with the break-up of a relationship or even the loss of a pet, the following spell will help to soothe savaged nerves.

YOU WILL NEED

Bach Rescue Remedy (available from most health food shops); frankincense oil; light tea made from rosehip or, better still, apothecary's rose petals (a handful of dried petals to 1 litre boiling water, brewed for 10 minutes); an unperfumed hand cream; 2 drops rose oil

THE FIRST THING YOU MUST DO TO CALM SOMEONE WHO IS HIGHLY NERVOUS IS TO MAKE THEM FEEL SECURE THOUGH NOT DETAINED: SIT THEM IN A SUPPORTIVE, ENVELOPING CHAIR, BUT GIVE THEM ROOM TO BREATHE. Your own movements must be as calm as possible and your voice hypnotically low and soothing. As soon as possible drip two or three drops of Bach Rescue Remedy on their tongue, then light the frankincense oil and brew the tea. Whilst you are waiting for it to steep, mix the hand cream with the rose oil and rub it very gently but firmly into the invalid's hands, massaging particularly at the wishbone joint between the thumb and index finger. Work continually, but don't appear hurried: your own calm, airy lightness of being will have a direct impact on the nerves of the patient. SERVE UP THE TEA (ADD HONEY IF NEED BE, AS SWEETNESS WILL HELP THE SHOCK) THEN START LAYING YOUR HANDS ON THEM: FIRST ON THEIR TEMPLES, THEN ON THEIR NECK, SHOULDERS AND ARMS. In each resting place, use all your mind power to inject gentle heat and light from your inner being into your friend. Imagine the light going right through their confused body, penetrating from each entry zone you touch. Do this for about ten minutes, whilst they sip at the tea. This is also a very good general tonic for older people and convalescents. When you have finished, wind the energy force down in your mind and imagine a very comforting hand slowly stroking their whole body. By all means actually do this if you feel you can. finally, just lay your right hand on his or her right lower arm; you should be able to feel your hand tingling slightly. If they now feel exhausted, encourage them to rest without moving too far. They will rouse themselves later feeling much more relaxed. DO THIS SEVERAL TIMES OVER A WEEK IF THE CONDITIONS INDICATE THAT IT WOULD BE BENEFICIAL.

Pet hypnosis ❦

HOW TO DEAL WITH A PSYCHOTIC PET. Pets are by no means the least important family members, and they should not be left out of the playful side of our magic. My daughter's pet rabbit behaves like a cat, lying on its back with paws in the air in front of the fire; a friend's budgerigar barks at their dog, and one of my neighbours has a huge old English sheep dog which is terrified of small dogs! So what can you do if your white cat wishes he was black?

If your pet has a nervous disposition which is spoiling their, or your, life, try the next spell to uncross their hooves or unruffle their whiskers.

YOU WILL NEED

Essential oils: melissa (lemon balm) oil if your pet is highly strung, clary sage if they are aggressive or hostile, bergamot if they seem despondent or depressed; a blue candle; catmint (25 g dried leaves or flowering tops); classical music (Mozart and Monteverdi recommended)

❦ FIRST YOU MUST CLEANSE THE ANIMAL'S SLEEPING QUARTERS, BY SENDING WHITE LIGHT IN A STRONG BEAM FROM YOUR MIND'S EYE AROUND THE WHOLE AREA. Next, take the chosen essential oil/s and sprinkle a couple of drops on their rug or cushion or whatever they sleep on. Pets have very sensitive noses and will sneeze if the dose is too direct or too strong. Burn a blue candle with your pet's eyes on the flame from time to time (it shouldn't be difficult to make them curious about what you're doing), and say a chant to both candle and pet: *Repeat their name three times followed by 'calm calm calm' several times.* ❦ GIVE YOUR PET A FEW CHOPPED-UP CATMINT LEAVES (NO PROBLEM FOR CATS, RABBITS, HAMSTERS, MICE ETC; FOR A DOG MAKE A LIGHT TEA AND COOL IT RIGHT DOWN, GIVING JUST A SMALL AMOUNT AS A DRINK). Catmint, apart from its notoriously aphrodisiac reputation for cats, is good for soothing fevers and has mild sedative properties which can even be used for children. finally, hold a music appreciation class for at least an hour a day for your pet: play some classical music very softly for them. This has more than a calming effect – some people say it improves the milk yield of cows and goats, and its effects on plants have been much discussed. Keep up this course of action over a week or so, and spend a certain amount of time stroking and playing with the animal beforehand. ❦ BECAUSE ANIMALS ARE SO VERY SENSITIVE, YOU MAY GET RESULTS FASTER WITH THEM THAN WITH ANY OTHER FAMILY MEMBER.

MIRROR MIRROR
ON THE WALL

A SELECTION OF SPELLS FOR HEALTH AND BEAUTY. The subject of health and magic is complex. Whilst the treatment of serious complaints is a matter for your doctor, I do feel that there are many minor ailments which can respond brilliantly to 'magic' – largely herbal medicines, but in some instances, a repetition of will (through chant or action) which is directing your body to rid itself of infection. I venture to say that this use of positive mind direction combined with conventional medicine may be helpful, too, in the treatment of more serious illnesses: it is surprising what a determined will can change.

All dolled up ● A WITCH'S POTION TO HELP SHED POUNDS.

YOU WILL NEED

25 g fennel seeds; patchouli oil; a 'poppet' (a doll to represent a person); fennel oil (optional)

● AS YOU ARE TRYING TO RID YOURSELF OF EXTRA WEIGHT, WORK ON A WANING MOON: MANY WOMEN BEGIN DIETS ON WAXING MOONS AND CAN'T UNDERSTAND WHY THEY CAN'T STAY WITH THEM. Make up a pot of fennel tea by steeping the seeds in half a litre of boiling water for 5 minutes, then drink it during the day. This age-old remedy is known to speed up the digestion of fatty foods and help sluggishness and flatulence. Taken in conjunction with a sensible eating regime it could make all the difference to staying with, and benefiting from, a slimming diet. Your doll is supposed to represent you. It could be bought or homemade, and you should dress it in clothes that represent you. It should start off swathed in layers of clothes; then each week, you remove an outer layer. This ritual is very important as it helps to channel your belief in yourself, and see yourself actually as a person of decreasing size. ● THE PATCHOULI OIL CAN BE BURNED DURING THE DAY, BUT IS EVEN MORE EFFECTIVE MASSAGED INTO THE BODY (ALWAYS DILUTE IN A BASE OIL: A FEW DROPS OF ESSENCE TO 10 ML ALMOND OIL). You could also add a few drops of fennel oil. When you have achieved your ideal size, place your slimmer doll in a key position in the kitchen or eating room; and reduce your intake of fennel tea to one cup a day.

To charm away warts ● THERE MUST BE MORE THAN A THOUSAND VARIATIONS OF WART-CHARMING SPELLS, BUT THIS ONE I HAVE FOUND TO BE RELIABLE AND EASY TO PERFORM!

YOU WILL NEED

A silver dish or bowl; some dandelions; lemon essential oil

● SINCE YOU ARE DRIVING THE WART AWAY, PERFORM THIS SPELL ON A WANING MOON. By moonlight, bathe the affected area in a silver dish half-filled with water into which you have placed some dandelions. Say the words: '*By the moon's eternal light, Drive away this ugly sight*'. Rub the dandelions onto the wart to release the sap and pat dry. It is traditional to bury the herbs, which you can do if you wish, otherwise just discard them. Last thing at night, dab some lemon essential oil neat onto the wart area. By morning you will see an improvement, and you should continue the use of the dandelions and the oil for the remainder of the waning moon. ● THE SAP FROM THE DANDELION HAS A PROVEN EFFECT ON WARTS.

To cure a cold ♥ THERE MUST BE AS MANY RECIPES FOR CURING THE COMMON COLD AS
THERE ARE WART INCANTATIONS, because until relatively recently a chill could be life-threatening. I've found the following
remedy to be effective.

YOU WILL NEED

*450 g fresh onions; ginger root; garlic; elderflowers (fresh if possible, otherwise a good commercial elderflower tea); honey if desired,
or if you have a cough as well; 2 teaspoons dry mustard powder; ginger and eucalyptus essential oils*

♥ TO HAVE THE BEST SUCCESS WITH THIS REMEDY YOU SHOULD BEGIN AS SOON AS YOU RECOGNISE COLD SYMPTOMS
STARTING: IN FACT, IF YOU GET IT EARLY ENOUGH, YOU CAN PREVENT THE ONSET ALTOGETHER. Take one onion and
quarter it, then place one quarter in each corner of your house to begin the battle against the spread of the infection.
With the remaining onions make up a French onion soup (don't take a short cut and use packet mixes) which you will sup on
through the course of a few days. Whilst your soup is cooking, make your herb tonic: grate some fresh ginger root and put it
with some crushed garlic into a mug; add the elderflowers (or elder tea) and steep for ten minutes before drinking. Add honey
if necessary. ♥ MEANWHILE, MAKE A HOT FOOT BATH BY ADDING THE DRY MUSTARD POWDER TO HOT WATER IN
A BASIN, AND SOAK YOUR FEET WHILST YOU SIP ON YOUR TEA. Sit somewhere comfortable and relax: experience the
wonderful warmth spreading from your feet, slowly up through your whole body, relaxing it, casting away tension, and driving
off the malady. Over a ten-minute period, try to feel your whole body glowing with warmth and triumphing over infection.

♥ DRINK YOUR TEA AND SOAK YOUR FEET THIS WAY TWO OR THREE TIMES IN THE DAY; AND FOLLOW THIS WITH
A LIGHT MEAL OF THE ONION SOUP. Wage this war for up to three days, and you should be the victor. During this period
burn the oils in the house; they will neutralise the sickness and you will absorb their healing essences.

The crystal beam ● A CANDLE-BURNING SPELL FOR SOMEONE IN NEED. When someone

you know and love is facing a serious illness or an operation, the use of energy transference can be a positive way of lending them some of your strength for their impending battle. You can do this quite effectively either at home or even by their hospital bed if you act quickly but stay calm.

YOU WILL NEED

A small crystal; a blue or green candle; 1 metre of green cord or ribbon; a pot of growing marigolds

● AS SOON AS YOU LEARN THAT YOUR LOVED ONE IS IN TROUBLE, BEGIN YOUR SPELL. Hold a small crystal in your right hand throughout the procedure and, when the spell is done, take it to your friend. If they are not near you, place it by a photo of them. ● LIGHT THE CANDLE AND SEE YOUR FRIEND'S FACE IN THE FLAME. Wind the cord around your left index finger and place it to your 'third eye'. Concentrate your energy on the person who is ill and look into the flame, still seeing their face there. Transfer all your own positive thought and energy to the patient, imagining the flame burning very brightly and then sending a beam of that light to them. Try to see them vividly in your mind, and swirl the light around their body in a halo of protection and energy. Concentrate these thoughts into the ribbon, and hold tightly to the crystal. Drum up as much mental energy as you can, and send it, like a beam, to your needy friend. Try gently to persuade them to fight their health problem with all their own strength and as much of yours as they can take; ask them to decide that they want to get well. ● SUSTAIN THIS FOR AS LONG AS YOU CAN, AND THEN TAKE THE CRYSTAL, THE RIBBON AND THE MARIGOLD PLANT TO THEM. Place the crystal under their pillow; tie the ribbon around the head of the bed in a bow; and place the flowers by the bedside (you may need to convince hospital staff that this is a religious ceremony of which the patient would approve). ● WHILST YOU KEEP VIGIL, SEND AS MUCH CONTINUED LIGHT AROUND THEIR BODY AS YOU CAN. It is now up to your loved one but, deep inside, they will have an extraordinary feeling of support.

Enchanted waters ☙ To cure aches and pains. Many people swear by the powers of natural

springs or holy wells to cure a range of illnesses. Healing waters seem to have had most success in helping muscular complaints and aches or skin disorders. If you have such a well-spring anywhere near your home, or if you want to try a commercial spring water poured into a silver dish, this is one of the most effective rituals for calling upon its powers to heal.

You will need

A few drops of frankincense and sandalwood essential oils diluted in 10 ml almond oil; 1 metre of green ribbon or cord;

holy or magic well water, or spring water in a silver bowl; a hazel twig or oak leaf; 9 g dried valerian root

☙ Choose a Sunday for performing this spell, and choose a moon appropriate to the problem. If you are casting off an ailment, use a waning moon; but if you are trying to invoke healing for a wound, you need an active, waxing moon. Anoint your wrists and forehead with the oil and tie the ribbon around the area needing treatment. Face the sun and ask for a healing force to drive away the negativity that has been dwelling in your body. Sprinkle a few drops of the water on your brow, and place the hazel twig or oak leaf in the water as an offering to the well. Now bathe the affected area and breathe the sunlight right into your system as you do so, asking it to dwell in the wound or penetrate the illness. Bathe the area three times, then remove the ribbon. Take some of the well water home with you in a small bottle to boil up and make an infusion with the valerian root. Soak the small amount of root in about 120 ml water for twelve hours, then for the next three days, at sunrise and sunset, tie the ribbon around the 'wound' again and drink some of the liquid. ☙ On the Thursday, return to the well and tie the ribbon around the tree nearest the water. You should notice a steady improvement from that day.

To cure a minor illness

♦ A RITUAL FOR PICKING AND CHARGING VERVAIN. This holy herb was renowned for centuries for its medicinal value and its magical properties. The Druids prized it as highly as their beloved mistletoe, and legend told that it was found on Mount Calvary and used to staunch Christ's wounds. ♦ VERVAIN HAS BEEN USED OVER THE YEARS TO KEEP EVIL SPIRITS FROM THE HOUSE, MIXED IN LOVE POTIONS, AND DRUNK AS A TEA FOR A HUNDRED COMPLAINTS. It is very refreshing if brewed in boiling water and then added to bath water. Use it as your intuition dictates and, whenever you gather it, say these enchanter's words: *'Oh healing hand, thou holy herb, Vervain, which groweth here upon the ground, Blessed be the field or lane, Where'er your leaf is found.'* ♦ You will find that 25 g dried leaves steeped in half a litre of boiling water relieves indigestion and upset stomachs; twice this strength is used to treat a cut or wound or burn and can be gargled for throat problems and mouth ulcers.

Lavender and basil

♦ TO CURE A HEADACHE. Lavender is well known for its relaxing properties, which may explain why it can help to cure tension headaches.

YOU WILL NEED

A sachet of dried lavender or a compress dipped in lavender oil; 1 metre of green ribbon; a basil leaf

♦ SMELL THE LAVENDER AND BREATHE ITS FRAGRANCE RIGHT INTO YOUR SYSTEM TO CLEANSE AND RELAX YOU (OR YOU CAN PLACE THE COMPRESS ON YOUR HEAD FOR A FEW MINUTES). Take your ribbon and wind it around the index finger of your left hand. Place it to your 'third eye' and gently rub back and forth over it. Now unwind the ribbon and wrap it around your forehead like a headband, securing a basil leaf under it over the third eye. Relax for ten minutes completely, and imagine the poisons draining out of your forehead into the ribbon. When you feel a lightening of the ache, remove the ribbon, cut it in half and discard it. This should lessen even a violent headache, and drive off a persistent one.

Top 10 witch's beauty tips

THE METEORIC RISE IN POPULARITY OF HERBAL POTIONS AND ESSENTIAL OILS CAN BE ATTESTED BY THE VARIETY OF PRODUCTS NOW ON THE MARKET. Almost wherever you live there is now someone specialising in selling flower- or herb-based lotions for skin, hair, nails and all varieties of cosmetic use. *Here is a more traditional selection of witchy tips.* To STAY YOUTHFUL: Macerate about a handful of the flowering tips and leaves of rosemary and marjoram in 300 ml of alcohol for a month; add honey and 2 tablespoons fresh blackcurrant juice; strain through a fine sieve and take 1/2 teaspoon two or three times a week. It also eases aches, strains and pains, and even helps with rheumatic disorders. To IMPROVE THE TEXTURE OF THE SKIN AND SOOTHE RASHES: Place the leaves and flowers of a handful of St John's Wort in a glass jar, just cover with olive or almond oil, stand for a month, strain, and use as a compress to treat rashes and inflammations. Some people develop a light sensitivity with this herb, so it is very important to remember not to go out in the sun directly after you have used it. To TREAT BURNS, SCALDS, SNAKE BITES AND SPOTS: Macerate 25 g fresh lavender flowers in 600 ml olive oil in the sunlight for three days, strain through a fine sieve or muslin and repeat the procedure for three more days. The highly perfumed oil should be stored in a dark glass bottle in a cool place and can be applied in small quantities as needed. To LIGHTEN FRECKLES: Crush some orris root to extract the juice and add to the bruised leaves of watercress; apply a small amount of the resulting liquid with a cotton bud. To AID IN THE ELIMINATION OF CELLULITE: Make a tea from 25 g meadowsweet flowers infused for 10 minutes in 600 ml not quite boiling water. Drink two cups of tea a day. Accompany this with massage of the affected areas using 10 ml almond oil, four drops cypress oil and two drops lemon essential oil. Treat for one month. To IMPROVE THE APPEARANCE OF DULL SKIN: Finely grind the flowering tops of evening primrose flowers, add to a paste made of almond oil and ground almonds, then apply as a face mask for ten minutes. This gives the skin a lovely radiance. To REDUCE HAIR LOSS: Prepare a tonic of 50 g nasturtium leaves, seeds and flowers, 25 g nettle leaves, two tablespoons marigold flowers, two tablespoons lavender flowers, four sprigs of rosemary and a handful of oak leaves all macerated for a month in 600 ml alcohol. Sieve three times, and use twice a week as a pre-shampoo treatment, leaving it on for at least 20 minutes. To IMPROVE CONDITION OF NAILS AND HAIR: Make a solution of lavender by steeping 10 flowering sprigs in 600 ml nearly boiling water for 30 minutes. Add one tablespoon of the resulting tonic to the pressed juice of herb watercress (*Nasturtium officinale*) and apply to the scalp and hair after shampoo and conditioning to strengthen and thicken it. Add a few drops to a hand cream and rub into the nails. Eat plenty of watercress and evening primrose (either in capsule form or by adding the flowers to salads) to increase the effect internally.

THE WILL TO SUCCEED

HOW TO GET AHEAD IN BUSINESS AND CLIMB THE LADDER OF SUCCESS. This chapter is a guide for those seeking prosperity and success. It is not a list of formulae for winning huge amounts of money, neither will it help if you expect life to provide for you without putting anything in on your own part. But it is a series of exercises to attract your share of luck and good will. Some people always seem to be in clover, with plenty of work, opportunities and prospects that appear to go from strength to strength. Try any of the following if you would join them.

Money to burn ● A CANDLE SPELL TO GET YOUR FINANCES MOVING.

YOU WILL NEED

Hyssop oil; a bunch of daisies; a green cloth; 1 metre of red ribbon; a green dinner candle; a bank note in any currency, worth about $1 U.S.

● WORK THIS SPELL ON A WAXING MOON AND PREFERABLY ON A THURSDAY OR, TO INFLUENCE A SPECIFIC CONTRACT OR TO AID IN BUYING PROPERTY, ON A SATURDAY. First prepare your altar, by burning some hyssop essential oil and placing some freshly cut daisies on a green cloth. Wind the red cord around the middle finger of your right hand and place on your breast. Concentrate all your force on attracting a busy, prosperous earning period ahead, and also, if you wish, on the possibility of gaining a bonus, such as a windfall or an unexpected lump sum, but do not allow greed to turn your head. Take the green candle and anoint it with hyssop oil, then light the candle with the money, and say: '*Within one week, Those things we seek, Will come within our power; All worries go, And money flow, In plenty from this hour.*' ● ASK YOUR PARTNER (BUSINESS OR LOVE) TO REPEAT THE VERSE WITH YOU A SECOND TIME IF YOU WANT TO ATTRACT GOOD LUCK AS A PAIR. Let the candle burn down safely during the course of the day, and keep just the stub (no more than 2.5 cm) tied with the red ribbon in a bow for a week after the spell, somewhere near, or on, the altar with the flowers. ● WITHIN THE WEEK, YOU SHOULD EXPERIENCE SOME PARTICULARLY UPLIFTING SIGNS IN BUSINESS THAT YOU DIDN'T ANTICIPATE OR, IF YOU ARE AWAITING THE OUTCOME OF A JOB INTERVIEW, YOU SHOULD GET THE ANSWER YOU WANT.

A variation on this spell can be done specifically on the eve of an important business venture or the launch of a project. Write the name of your company and/or partners, or just a short description of the business plan you are unfolding, on a piece of green paper. Add a drop or two of hyssop oil to it, then wrap it up inside the money and continue in the same way, burning names and cash together as you light the candle. At the end of the ritual, when you are tying the ribbon around the candle stump, write again the name of your venture or partners, and attach them to the candle inside the ribbon. Keep this safe in a small pouch until the venture has succeeded.

To climb the corporate ladder ● A SPELL SPECIALLY FORMULATED

FOR SWIFT PROGRESS AT WORK. This spell has two real applications. If you are just starting a new job you should perform this ceremony on the first day, when you return from work. Alternatively, it would be appropriate to use this spell if you are opening a small business, such as a shop, in a field in which there are many other competitors.

YOU WILL NEED

An acorn; a Chinese jade tree, planted in a green pot; a small step-ladder

● WHEN YOU COLLECT YOUR ACORN, TOUCH THE OAK TREE AND ASK FOR ITS BLESSING, AND POUR A SMALL CUP OF ALE OR WINE AROUND ITS ROOTS. Having done this before you start the job, take the acorn with you in your pocket for the whole of the first day, and touch it each time you are introduced to someone new or go into a new room or work area. At the end of the working day, go back to your home and place the jade tree at your front door. Push the acorn into the soil around the jade tree and say: *'My talents all shall blossom forth, My skills be in demand; And from this day promotion shall, With luck, go hand in hand.'* Place the little plant at the front door on a small step-ladder, by way of an unusual plant-holder; if you like, arrange other plants on the lower steps, but the jade tree must go at the top. ● IF YOU LIVE IN A WARM ENOUGH CLIMATE FOR THE JADE TREE TO LIVE OUTSIDE, OMIT THE LADDER AND PLANT IT ON HIGH GROUND, OR PLACE IT ON A TOP STEP. Keep the plant healthy and well and you will meet with much success in your chosen career. If you have a front and a back door, work the spell with two trees and two acorns, placing one tree at either door.

Busy as a bee ❦ A SPELL TO BRING IN MORE WORK. This spell must be the automatic choice if you're usually inundated with work but, for some reason, things have recently gone a little flat and you're not as busy as you'd like to be. This is like a secret telegraph wire that sends your full page advertisement into the ether.

YOU WILL NEED

Your business card; a pen; a bag of pleated cotton wool; a 30 cm length of red ribbon; a small frosted glass bottle with stopper; a jar of honey.

❦ FOR THIS SPELL TO WORK BEST YOU SHOULD CHOOSE A WAXING MOON, PREFERABLY A BRAND NEW ONE. Sit calmly, with your ingredients in front of you, and strongly visualise your happiest moments of industry. See yourself busy with a challenging workload and any others around you also cheerfully employed with work they're happy to do. Consider briefly whether, in the past, you've sometimes been so flat out to meet deadlines that you've been unable to eat properly, or complained that there simply weren't enough hours in the day. Make a mental note to correct this imbalance, to make time for those who are important to you and never again to complain about having too much to do. Say out loud: *'My life and accounts shall soon be in balance'*, and pick up your business card. Use the pen to draw on the back of the card a simple picture of a busy bee, buzzing from flower to flower. Imagine yourself in the same role, happy in your work. ❦ LAY THE CARD ON A PLEAT OF COTTON WOOL, AND ROLL THEM INTO A SMALL, CYLINDRICAL SHAPE, REPEATING THE WORDS ABOVE AS YOU DO THIS. Using the red ribbon, tie the little scroll up with a small neat bow and post it through the mouth of the bottle, then fill it to the brim with honey. Place the stopper in the top repeating the words above. If you live in the country or have a small garden, you should now dig a hole to plant a baby oak tree, putting the bottle underneath and saying: *'My life and accounts shall soon be in balance, and my house and happiness shall flourish'*. If you cannot plant a tree, or live in an apartment in town, say the same words whilst placing the bottle in your freezer. Every evening whilst the moon is still waxing, either water your oak or turn your bottle clockwise in the freezer, repeating the words as you do this. ❦ DON'T LET YOUR TREE GO THIRSTY, OR YOUR FREEZER DEFROST, AND BY THE NEXT NEW MOON, THINGS SHOULD HAVE PICKED UP CONSIDERABLY.

'Sugar & spice & all things nice' ♥ To ATTRACT A SHOWER OF GIFTS.

This spell is for those who would love to be given items of value by their lovers; but remember, this is no measure of true love. The sugar in the spell represents exotic spices from faraway lands and the pearls, treasures from deep and secret places.

YOU WILL NEED

A golden candle (the colour must be true gold, rather than yellow); benzoin oil; some sugar; a string of pearls

♥ ON A THURSDAY NIGHT NEAR TO A FULL MOON, ROLL THE CANDLE IN BENZOIN OIL AND THEN IN SUGAR. Allow the sugar to dry hard on the candle, then place it in your special holder. Wind the string of pearls around the bottom of the candle holder, then light the candle. As it begins to burn, say: *'I am precious, My love too; What real value, Have I for you?'* Sit well back as the candle burns as it might spit a little with the burning sugar. Keep a close eye on the candle whilst it burns down, repeating the words at regular intervals. ♥ THIS SPELL SHOULD BRING INTERESTING RESULTS. Whilst it may not provide you with a millionaire, you may find that your previously undemonstrative lover starts to bring you little gifts.

An extraordinarily literal result of this spell for my girlfriend Lucy was a regular invitation to holiday in the West Indies where coincidentally (or not!) sugar is produced.

Walk on gold ❦ A MONEY TALISMAN TO BE IN THE HABIT OF USING. Certain lucky charms seem

to have a proven effect in bringing many small parcels of prosperity over a continuing period of time. In many respects this is greatly to be preferred to a larger sum which is here today and gone all too soon. Try either or both of the following spells if you would like to be a person whose luck with money and business success just keeps ticking over nicely.

YOU WILL NEED

A 'gold' coin (gold coloured will do); a cotton wool pad if needed

❦ THIS PRACTICE WAS LONG REGARDED BY WISE WOMEN AS THE BEST WAY OF ENSURING THERE IS ALWAYS MONEY IN AN EMERGENCY. It became so settled in the imagination that, ultimately, it found its way into wedding ceremonies in the rhyme: *'Something old, Something new, Something borrowed, Something blue. And a silver sixpence in your shoe.'* The original practice was to put a piece of gold in your shoe, first showing it to the sun and asking his blessing that your fortunes would from this day forward be surrounded in a glow of golden brightness. As you do so you should say the words: *'I need no jewels nor bags of gold; But may my purse have enough to hold'.* ❦ IF THE COIN FEELS UNCOMFORTABLE, COVER IT WITH A COTTON PAD AND SECURE IT WHERE IT WILL NOT CAUSE A BLISTER; pop your lucky coin in your shoe as often as possible and be careful never to spend it.

Silvery moon ❦ FOR THIS MONEY CHARM YOU NEED TO ORDER A SPECIAL PIECE OF SILVER

WHICH SYMBOLISES THE FRUITS OF SUCCESS. This should be a personal choice, and good examples of appropriate symbols would be any nut or fruit to symbolize the harvest, an ear of corn or a peony flower.

YOU WILL NEED

A piece of personally commissioned silver to charge with the moon's rays

❦ KEEP YOUR PIECE OF SILVER IN A SMALL POUCH UNTIL THE NIGHT YOU CHARGE IT WITH THE MOON'S LIGHT, WHICH SHOULD BE ON ONE OF THE FOLLOWING DATES: LAMMAS (AUGUST 1), BELTANE (MAY 1), ROWAN DAY (MAY 13), MIDSUMMER DAY (JUNE 21), OR ST SWITHIN'S DAY (JULY 15). Place the silver on your forehead, then hold it up to the moon and draw the tide of her magnetic power into the metal, saying: *'May my fortunes grow from this day.'* Wear the charm somewhere close to you, but not on public view (even on a key chain is fine). Touch the talisman and look to the moon whenever you need special help.

Hot wax

◆ A RITUAL TO ENSURE YOUR BEST CHANCE OF SUCCESS BEFORE A PRIZE DRAW. If you are hoping to win a bonus of money in a prize draw, sweepstake or lottery, here is a spell you can do to improve your chances: but remember that balance is part of the creed of magic, *and greed is not!* If you have a good purpose in mind, and plan to distribute some of your winnings in one or two other charitable directions, you may meet with more success than someone who is motivated by pure selfishness. Remember, too, that scale is relative; you will be considered lucky to win £500, despite the fact that you might wish to make the sum ten times greater.

YOU WILL NEED

Peony, hyssop or frankincense oil; a red or gold dinner candle; a pin or sharp-pointed pen; gold cord

◆ THIS SPELL MUST BE PERFORMED ON A WAXING MOON. If you were to do the spell on a waning moon the opposite might happen and you might find yourself instead the recipient of masses of mysterious bills! Before you begin the spell you should burn some prosperity-related oil or scent to attract finances to your home: peony is the best for this, but hyssop and frankincense are also good. If you are inspired by Oriental ideology, make almond essence your choice. ◆ TAKE YOUR CANDLE AND WARM IT FIRST, EITHER OVER ANOTHER CANDLE'S FLAME OR ON A WARM SURFACE, SO THAT THE WAX DOWN ONE EDGE IS SOFT AND PLIABLE. Take your sharp implement and write your name in flowing script down the soft edge of the candle. Light the candle and see the bright glow of success and delight in its flame: imagine you are surprised by winning a prize or cash bonus. As you watch the flame burn down, make a pledge about what you would do if favoured with lucky money, and only make promises you know you could keep; *please don't be greedy and think of large sums.* During the ceremony, rise and make your pledge also to the moon, and do not specify a date or time by which you ask to be favoured. After the candle has burned down to the stump, extinguish it and take it with you, tied with gold cord, to buy your ticket or enter your draw. ◆ IF YOUR PLEDGE HAS BEEN SEEN AS SINCERE, YOU MAY MEET WITH EXTRAORDINARY GOOD FORTUNE.

Many people prefer to do this spell in stages, burning it three times to equal notches over the course of the waxing moon, until the day just before full. This means you might be preparing for luck at any stage, and your chances will be even stronger.

GOOD LUCK
& BEST
WISHES

Amulets and spells to attract luck & protect home family & friends. Luck may be just a matter of recognition. If we are well throughout most of the year, drive a car without having an accident, and have children who are for the most part healthy and whole, we are abundantly lucky. But there are degrees of luck, and it is my belief that a cheerful and positive mind goes a long way towards attracting the good things in life. If your luck could do with a boost, try some of these spells.